Life in the Midwest

Zachary Everson

Series Editor
Mark Pearcy

Contents

Shaping the Midwest

The American Midwest is a diverse region. It includes plains, forests, farmlands, and huge lakes. It is also home to many peoples with unique cultures. There are 12 states and several major cities in the Midwest.

The first people to live in the Midwest were the American Indians. They have lived in the region for thousands of years. French explorers were the first Europeans to reach the Midwest. Later, people from Finland, Germany, Ireland, Norway, and Sweden arrived in the region.

New industries soon formed in the Midwest. This attracted new people to the region in search of work. For example, the fur trade around the Great Lakes led to new settlements. It also led to trade between different peoples.

In 2017, the **population** of the Midwest was more than 68 million. This includes **indigenous** people, migrants from other states, and immigrants from around the world. People have come from countries such as China, India, Iraq, Laos, Lebanon, Mexico, the Philippines, Somalia, and Vietnam.

This book takes a look at how diverse peoples, industries, and cultures have shaped the Midwest over the years.

For Your Information

The 12 states of the Midwest are Michigan, Ohio, Indiana, Wisconsin, Illinois, Minnesota, Iowa, Missouri, North Dakota, South Dakota, Nebraska, and Kansas.

American Indians

The Midwest is home to many American Indian peoples. Many Midwestern places are named after American Indian words.

American Indians of the Great Plains

The Great Plains region is home to several American Indian peoples, including the Iowa, Omaha, and Lakota. The Lakota have lived in the area for thousands of years. They settled near the Black Hills around the late 1700s. In 1886, the U.S. government took over the Black Hills. They forced the Lakota out of the area. The Lakota have been fighting for the return of their land ever since. The U.S. government offered $102 million to the Lakota in 1980. But the Lakota rejected this offer. They believe that the land should be given back to them.

The Black Hills mountain range is covered in trees. The trees make the mountains look black from far away.

A Disputed Monument

The Crazy Horse Memorial is an unfinished statue in the Black Hills. It has been under construction since 1948. If it is ever completed, it will be the largest sculpture in the world. It was designed by a Polish American sculptor. The sculpture is of a famous Lakota leader named Crazy Horse. He is looking over the land and pointing with his index finger. However, American Indians traditionally did not point in this way. Because of this, many American Indians have spoken out against the memorial.

Cahokia

The Mississippian people built the city of Cahokia around the year 700. Cahokia was located near modern-day St. Louis, Missouri. Workers built 120 huge mounds out of soil. One of the remaining mounds is 100 feet tall and more than 14 acres in size. Historians believe that temples were built on top of the mounds. Cahokia was **abandoned,** but experts are not sure why.

American Indians of the Great Lakes

Some of the American Indian peoples who live in the Great Lakes region include the Ojibwa, Sauk, Fox, Potawatomi, and Erie.

For Your Information

Some American Indian peoples living around the Great Lakes today did not always live there. They were forced to move there by the U.S. government. For example, in the 1830s, most of the Illinois Indians were forced out of the Central Plains. The government made them move to an area near Lake Erie.

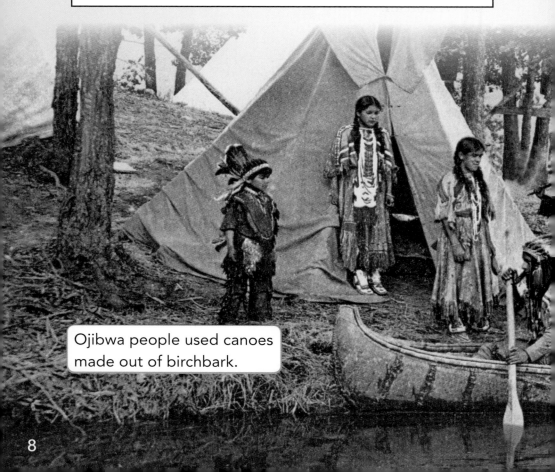

Ojibwa people used canoes made out of birchbark.

The Menominee and Ojibwa have hunted and fished in the Great Lakes region for thousands of years. These activities are very important to the American Indians of the Great Lakes. In fact, the Menominee celebrate when sturgeon swim back to the region to **spawn.** They celebrate the beginning of spring with singing and dancing. They also enjoy traditional foods such as wild rice, smoked fish, and maple sugar.

However, the U.S. government took over many traditional hunting and fishing grounds. But Great Lakes Indians won back some of their traditional fishing areas in 1983. These areas are in Michigan, Minnesota, and Wisconsin.

Growth and Change

Some areas of the Midwest have nicknames based on their main industries. For example, the Corn Belt is an area of the Great Plains that is named after all the corn farms found there. And Kansas is called the Wheat State because of its grain farms.

Car production in the early 1900s created many jobs for people in the Midwest. Detroit, Michigan, was the center of the country's auto industry. It became known as Motor City.

Changing Industries

Industries in the Midwest have changed over the years. Some factories are using machines to replace human jobs. Other factories have had to close. This has affected many cities. Some people are moving away from these cities to find jobs in other areas.

Many factories in the Midwest have closed over the years.

The Rust Belt is an area of the Great Lakes where industries have suffered. Cities in the area have been worn down by job loss. This is similar to how rust wears down a car.

However, people in the Midwest are starting new industries. These industries create jobs and help to restore the economy. Cleveland has built a major healthcare industry. This has attracted many people to the city.

Renewable energy is another new industry in the Midwest. Minnesota is now a major producer of solar power. Iowa is a major producer of wind power. The renewable energy industry has created more than half a million jobs in the Midwest.

There are now many wind farms in the Midwest.

Music and Comedy

The Midwest is home to many **iconic** musical styles. It has also contributed to the art of comedy.

Blues

Blues can be traced back to the first enslaved Africans in America. They brought unique musical traditions with them from Africa. These traditions were used to create songs called spirituals. These songs reflected the hardship that enslaved people faced. Eventually, new instruments were added to the spirituals. This was the beginning of blues music.

Blues reached the Midwest in the early 1900s. In St. Louis, blues was combined with upbeat ragtime music. In Chicago, electric guitars and harmonicas were added to blues. Chicago blues reflected life in the big city.

Muddy Waters was a famous blues musician who lived in Chicago.

The Jackson 5 was a famous Motown group.

Motown

Blues paved the way for R&B, or rhythm and blues.
A Detroit record label called Motown Records began
releasing catchy R&B music in 1959. The music released
by Motown Records became very popular. It soon
became its own genre. This is how Motown was born.

Motown music was a catchy blend of gospel music and
R&B. It pushed many African American performers to
national **stardom.** During this time, many concert
venues were **segregated** by race. However, Detroit's
Motown scene brought music fans of different races
together. The Supremes, the Jackson 5, Marvin
Gaye, and Stevie Wonder gained fame through their
Motown sound.

13

Hip-Hop

Hip-hop is a popular genre in Chicago. Common was one of the first Chicago rappers to be famous outside Chicago. The positive messages in his music helped him to stand out from other rappers. Kanye West is another important figure in Chicago hip-hop. West's music includes elements of different musical styles, such as electronic dance music. Today, he is one of the most well-known rappers in the world. Another Chicago artist, Chance the Rapper, mixes jazz and gospel in his music. He also promotes a positive message in his lyrics.

Kanye West has won many awards for his music.

Improv Comedy

Improv, or improvisational, comedy was born in the Midwest. It was developed in Chicago in the 1950s. Improv performers do not use a script. They ask the audience for ideas for scenes. Then they act out the scenes without preparation.

The Second City® is a theater company that started in Chicago. It helped to make improv popular. Many comedians and actors travel to Chicago to train with the Second City. In fact, late-night TV host Stephen Colbert trained at the Second City. Writer, producer, and actor Tina Fey also trained at the Second City.

Tina Fey

Stephen Colbert

Stories From the Midwest

The Midwest is also home to many famous authors. Some of these authors use their writing to point out problems in society. Upton Sinclair worked in Chicago's meat industry in the early 1900s. He used this experience to write *The Jungle.* This novel is about an immigrant working in a difficult and dangerous meatpacking job. The novel caused people to demand new food safety laws.

Upton Sinclair

Willa Cather was another Midwestern author. She wrote about life in rural Nebraska. Many people could relate to her books. One of her most famous books, *My Ántonia,* is about a boy and a girl who move to Nebraska.

Willa Cather

Laura Ingalls Wilder's *Little House on the Prairie* is a series of books about life in rural Wisconsin and Kansas. These books were written in the early 1900s. They were adapted into a popular TV series in the 1970s.

Laura Ingalls Wilder

Kurt Vonnegut grew up in Indiana. He wrote novels and essays that criticized war and inequality in America. His novels used science fiction as a creative way to expose issues facing Americans.

Kurt Vonnegut

Maya Angelou was another Midwestern author who wrote about issues in America. She promoted equality in books such as *I Know Why the Caged Bird Sings.* This novel is about her experiences as a young African American girl.

Maya Angelou

Cuisine

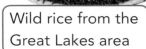

Before Europeans arrived, American Indians relied mostly on resources that were available around them. Wild rice was common around the Great Lakes. It was a **staple** food

Wild rice from the Great Lakes area

for the Menominee and other Great Lakes Indians. In fact, *Menominee* means "people of the wild rice" in Ojibwa.

Many people who moved to the Midwest brought their culture's cuisine with them. Northern Europeans brought lefse, a flatbread made from potatoes. They also brought lutefisk, a dried fish soaked in **lye.** German immigrants brought sausages called bratwursts and a cabbage dish called sauerkraut.

Chinese and Mexican restaurants are common in the Midwest. Tibetan food has become popular in Bloomington, Indiana. And Lebanese immigrants have brought their cuisine to Detroit.

Many different cuisines have been brought to the Midwest over the years.

Local Favorites

Different regions in the Midwest have dishes that are local favorites. For example, Chicago is known for its deep-dish pizza.

Cheese curds

St. Louis has its own style of barbecue. In Southern barbecue, meats are smoked or slow-cooked. However, in St. Louis barbecue, meats are grilled and covered in a special sauce.

Cheese curds are squeaky bits of cheese that are popular in Wisconsin. Fresh cheese curds make a squeaky sound when they are bitten.

Buckeyes are a local favorite in Ohio. They are a combination of peanut butter and chocolate. Buckeye treats look like the nuts of the buckeye tree.

Chicago deep-dish pizza

Visiting the Midwest

There are many reasons that people visit the Midwest. Natural features and human-made attractions bring many people to the Midwest.

Natural Features

The Midwest has a diverse geography. The Black Hills region has high mountain peaks. It also has deep valleys and dense forests. Nebraska's Sand Hills are sand dunes that are covered in prairie grasses.

The Great Lakes hold one fifth of the world's surface fresh water. They form the largest fresh water system in the world. Common activities for visitors include hiking, camping, fishing, and water-skiing.

The Midwest is also home to a large part of the Mississippi River. This river is more than 2,000 miles long.

Nebraska's Sand Hills area is a national landmark.

There are hundreds of different stores in the Mall of America®.

Human-Made Attractions

The Mall of America in Minnesota was the largest shopping mall in the country when it was finished in 1992. It contains a theme park and an aquarium. More than 40 million people visit this mall every year.

For Your Information

Wisconsin Dells is famous for its many water parks. Noah's Ark® Water Park in Wisconsin Dells is considered the largest water park in the United States.

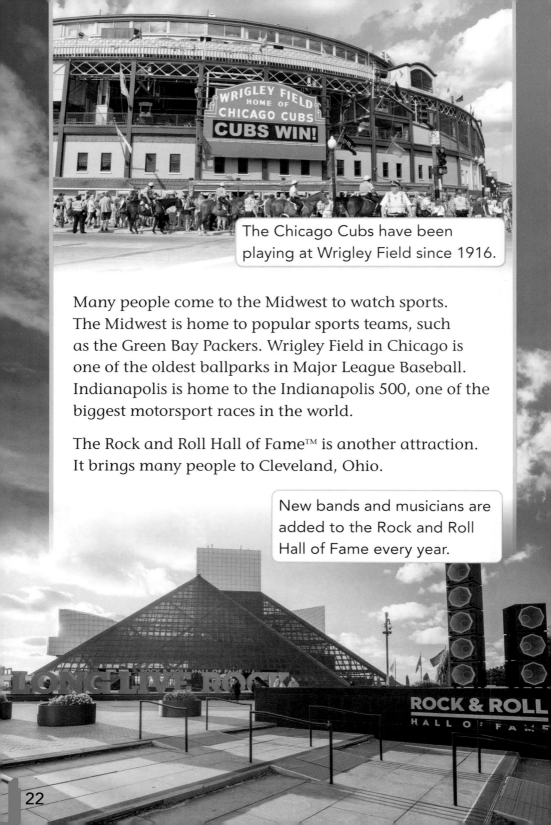

The Chicago Cubs have been playing at Wrigley Field since 1916.

Many people come to the Midwest to watch sports. The Midwest is home to popular sports teams, such as the Green Bay Packers. Wrigley Field in Chicago is one of the oldest ballparks in Major League Baseball. Indianapolis is home to the Indianapolis 500, one of the biggest motorsport races in the world.

The Rock and Roll Hall of Fame™ is another attraction. It brings many people to Cleveland, Ohio.

New bands and musicians are added to the Rock and Roll Hall of Fame every year.

A Region Shaped by Change

The Midwest is a diverse region with many cultures and geographical features. The area has changed a lot over the years. New people have moved to the Midwest, and new industries have been developed there. These events have shaped the cuisine, music, and literature of the Midwest.

Has the area where you live changed over the years? Think about the foods and styles of music that are popular in your community. Also think about the industries and tourist attractions in the area. All of these things help to shape the unique regions of the United States.

Glossary

abandon: to desert or leave forever

iconic: well-known and admired

indigenous: native to a particular area

lye: a substance made from wood ashes that can be used to preserve food

population: the number of people who live in an area

segregate: to separate based on race

spawn: to lay eggs

staple: dependable; important to life in a certain community

stardom: a position of fame

Index